F.

D0888032

Chazz Palminteri

SAMUEL FRENCH, INC.
45 West 25th Street   NEW YORK 10010
7623 Sunset Boulevard HOLLYWOOD 90046
LONDON   TORONTO

IMPORTANT BILLING AND CREDIT
REQUIREMENTS

All producers of *FAITHFUL must* give credit to the Author of the Play in all programs distributed in connection with performances of the Play and in all instances in which the title of the Play appears for purposes of advertising, publicizing or otherwise exploiting the Play and/or a production. The name of the Author *must* also appear on a separate line, on which no other name appears, immediately following the title, and *must* appear in size of type not less than fifty percent the size of the title type.

FAITHFUL premiered at The Court Theatre in California in 1991. It was produced by Gatien-Lauria, directed by Mark W. Travis and had the following cast:

JACK ....James Handy
MARGARET..Bridget Hanley
TONY ....Chazz Palminteri

Stage Manager: Peter DeAnella
Art Director/Set Design: Kathleen B. Cooper
Lighting Design: Ken Booth
Music/Sound Design: Alphonse Ranaudo

CHARACTERS

JACK

MARGARET

TONY (MAN)

TIME & PLACE

A mansion somewhere in upstate New York

ACT I
The Present, late afternoon

ACT II
Later that same evening

ACT I

A beautifully furnished living room with high ceilings, thick carpeting, and a large arched doorway. This is obviously the main sitting room of a very wealthy estate. Upstage, there are French windows leading out to a garden patio with fountains and statues. Stage right is the main entrance, large heavy doors that lead not outside, but to another internal hallway. Center stage is a very comfortable couch with glass coffee table. Stage left is an ornate, French provincial desk, with phone. Above a credenza up stage left is a bank of television monitors, revealing the images recorded by many security cameras all over the estate. The room is decorated with all the current fashionable works of art. A WOMAN in her mid-forties is tied in the desk chair (on wheels) in the center of the room.

As the LIGHTS COME UP: A MAN in his late thirties, dressed impeccably, is standing over her.

MAN. Faithful. You shoulda been faithful. If a guy's married, but he's ugly, and he can't get anybody else, does that make him faithful? If a woman is afraid to cheat on her husband because she knows he'll kill her if he finds out. Does that really make her faithful?... No ... Faithful is when you've got more to lose than gain ... You think about doing it, but you don't cheat. I mean, it's unnatural being with the same person for the rest of your life. You know, my uncle got divorced after forty-seven years? Forty-seven years. I asked him one day why he did it. I'll never forget it. He was sitting at the kitchen table having coffee. I walked over to him and said: "Uncle Vinnie, why after forty-seven years you're getting a divorce?" He took a sip of coffee, put the cup down, looked me square in the eyes, and said: "Because I fuckin' hate her." Forty-seven years, and now he hates her. He handed me his watch and said: "You see this watch? Look at the crystal. It's cracked. It's been cracked for twenty years. You know how I cracked it?" I said: "How?" He told me he threw a punch at my aunt and missed her and hit the refrigerator, but he never got it fixed, because every time he looks at his watch during the day, he wants it to remind him of how much he fuckin' hates her. Faithful. You shoulda been faithful.

MARGARET. What's your name?

MAN. What?

MARGARET. I said, what's your name?

MAN. None of your fuckin' business.

MARGARET. You're afraid, aren't you?

MAN. I'm not afraid of nothin'.

MARGARET. Yes you are. You're afr—

MAN. Tony, my name is Tony, it doesn't matter anyway 'cause you're gonna be dead soon.

MARGARET. "Tony" ... your name is Tony and you're in the mafia and you're a hit man ... how common.

TONY. You shoulda been faithful.

MARGARET. Faithful?... What the hell are you talking about? I did nothing, my husband's the one who's been unfaithful. I know all about his little love affairs, he's been cheating on me for twenty years.

TONY. And you never did nothing?

MARGARET. I went to dinner with a gentleman.

TONY. All right, now the truth comes out.

MARGARET. Look, I admit that I wanted to have an affair but I couldn't do it. The guy took me back to his apartment and he wanted to make love to me. But I couldn't do it. I couldn't even kiss him. Twenty years my husband's been cheating on me and I couldn't even do it once.

TONY. You're stupid.

MARGARET. What?

TONY. You're stupid. Twenty years he's been doin' it to you and you had a shot and didn't do it? Bad move.

MARGARET. *(Beat.)* Have you ever been in love.

TONY. Yeah, I've been in love?

MARGARET. What happened?

TONY. It didn't work out.

MARGARET. Why?

TONY. I had to kill her father.

MARGARET. Well I can see why it didn't work out.

TONY. Hey, I was honest with her.

MARGARET. Were you faithful?

TONY. Well kind of. Of.

MARGARET. What do you mean "kind of"? You either are, or you aren't.

TONY. Yeah. I was faithful. I was faithful for six weeks.

MARGARET. Six weeks?

TONY. Yeah, to me that's a long time. Wait a minute. When I was married, I was faithful for two years.

MARGARET. Two years? That's pretty good.

TONY. Yeah, I was faithful for two years. *(Beat.)* Not counting blow Jobs.

MARGARET. Blow jobs?

TONY. Well, I would get blowed by other women, but blow jobs don't count.

MARGARET. Let me get this straight, blow jobs, oral sex … that doesn't count?

TONY. Absolutely not.

MARGARET. Haven't you ever been in real love? Got a warm feeling in your heart. Didn't you ever feel real passion?

TONY. What?

MARGARET. Never mind.

TONY. (*Beat.*) Did you get married in church?

MARGARET. Did I what?

TONY. When you and your husband got married was it in church?

MARGARET. Yes.

TONY. Wow.

MARGARET. What's a matter?

TONY. Nothing.

MARGARET. What do you mean nothing? You ask me a question like that and then you say wow … what does wow mean?

TONY. Wow means how could two people fall in love, get married before God and then one of them pays a stranger to kill the other, that's what wow means.

MARGARET. Did you get married in church?

TONY. Yeah.

MARGARET. You took an oath before God?

TONY. Yeah.

MARGARET. Well let me ask you something. When you were married, if your wife went down on another man, that would be okay? That wouldn't be cheating? I mean that's what you said, right?

TONY. You're really hung up on this blow job thing. Are you comin' on to me? 'Cause if you are forget it. Don't even think about it. I was paid good money to kill you.

MARGARET. How much?

TONY. A lot.

MARGARET. I can give you a great deal of money.

TONY. Forget it. A deal's a deal. I never go back on my word.

MARGARET. I'm talking about one hundred thousand dollars.

TONY. No. You're husband hired me because I'm the best. I have a reputation of a man who gets the job done and never goes back on his word, I can't let you go.

MARGARET. I'm not asking you to let me go. You can still kill me. Look, I have a lot of money in the safe and I'm willing to give you the combination. Just tell me that when I die, that son of a bitch is going to die right after me.

TONY. How do you know I won't take the money after you're dead and not kill him?

MARGARET. You won't. You'll kill him.

TONY. What makes you so sure?

MARGARET. Because you're a man of your word. Give me your word that you'll do it. C'mon, Tony. One hundred thousand dollars. Think about it. Sun and fun and all the blow jobs you want.

TONY. I'll think about it.

(The TELEPHONE on a side table rings. TONY tenses and begins to move towards Margaret. For the first time we

see the gun stuck in his waistband. MARGARET watches him as HE listens intently to the PHONE ring once, twice ... and then on the third ring HE suddenly relaxes and begins to move away from her.)

MARGARET. Getting nervous?

TONY. Just waiting for a call.

MARGARET. From who?

TONY. Your husband.

MARGARET. My husband is going to call here? I want to talk to him.

TONY. Well he doesn't want to talk to you. Right now he's getting himself a nice alibi. He's driving upstate and when he gets far enough away, he's gonna call and signal me by letting the phone ring twice. That's when you die, Maggie.

MARGARET. Maggie?

TONY. This is 375 Chestnut Drive, right?

MARGARET. Maggie?

TONY. That's your name right?

MARGARET. Yes, but my father's the only one who ever called me Maggie. I'm named after his mother, but he never liked the name Margaret.

TONY. That's weird. My mother's the only one who ever called me Anthony. She always said Tony sounded like a hoodlum's name.

MARGARET. Is your mother still alive?

TONY. Whatta you want from me?

MARGARET. I don't want anything.

TONY. (*Walks over to a wet bar. HE pulls a pair of leather gloves out of jacket and slips them on.*) Then why do you keep asking me questions? You sound like my shrink.

MARGARET. You're in therapy?

TONY. Yeah, so what … I'm not ashamed to say I got problems like anybody else. (*TONY fixes himself a drink.*)

MARGARET. Look I didn't mean to offend you, I have problems too. I've been seeing a therapist for the past five years, but you're a hired killer.

TONY. It's a job.

MARGARET. A job? You take human life. What does your therapist say about that?

TONY. What's he gonna say?

MARGARET. That it's wrong. Aren't you afraid he'll tell the police?

TONY. He can't tell anybody. A shrink can't tell anybody what goes on between him and a patient. It's confidential.

MARGARET. But not when it comes to murder.

TONY. That's right, he also knows I'll fuckin' kill him if he opens his mouth.

MARGARET. Have you been seeing him a long time?

TONY. Three years and it hasn't cost me a dime.

MARGARET. Why not?

TONY. My shrink is a degenerate gambler. He grew up in my neighborhood. I set him up with my cousin who's a bookmaker. The Doc is a born loser. He couldn't pick his own birthday. I see him twice a week on the house. It's the barter system.

MARGARET. Your therapist sounds like a very reputable person.

TONY. You making fun of him? Everybody's got problems, baby. Look at you. You got all the money in the world and it didn't make you happy. Money makes it worst.

MARGARET. Why?

TONY. Because it takes away all your problems. Then you got nothing to worry about, you got no choice but to look inside yourself and see how fucked up you are, money changes people usually for the worst.

MARGARET. Money made my husband worse, but he's always been unfaithful.

TONY. It's impossible for a man to be faithful to a woman today.

MARGARET. You're wrong. My father was faithful to my mother all his life.

TONY. It was different back then.

MARGARET. Why?

TONY. Let me teach you something about marriage. Hundreds and hundreds of years ago when this thing called marriage was invented, it was easy for a man to be faithful to one woman.

MARGARET. Why?

TONY. Because men only lived to be forty years old. It was easier back then.

MARGARET. Wait a minute, let me get this straight. It's because men live longer today, that's why they can't be faithful to one woman?

TONY. No.

MARGARET. Then what's the reason?

TONY. There are too many cocktail waitresses today.

MARGARET. You don't trust women do you?

TONY. I don't trust nobody.

MARGARET. You need help.

TONY. No baby you got it wrong, you're tied up, you're the one who needs help. Don't you see what's happening here? I was sent here by your husband to kill you, to leave you dead and bleeding like some fuckin' animal. I was told to make it look like a rape and murder. Do you know there's an insurance policy on you?

MARGARET. I know. It's for a million dollars but my husband would never kill me just for money.

TONY. Oh no? People die for a lot less, baby.

MARGARET. It's not the money.

TONY. Then what is it?

MARGARET. Debbie.

TONY. Who the fuck is Debbie?

MARGARET. She works for my husband. She started out as just one of the secretaries at the plant but after six months she became his personal assistant.

TONY. Same old story. How'd you find out?

MARGARET. Easy guess. No brains, big tits ... probably fake. Jack was always a sucker for a beautiful woman. There should be a law against twenty-four-year-olds with big tits named Debbie. My husband wants it all, the money and the girl. I was a fool. We've been together so long, I thought no matter what he would always love me.

TONY. (*Laughs.*) Well maybe he loves you but he's not in love with you.

MARGARET. What's so funny?

TONY. Some broad told me that once. "I love you but I'm not in love with you." To me it's a nice way of telling someone to go fuck yourself.

MARGARET. That woman hurt you, didn't she?

TONY. I found her in bed with my best friend. They were fuckin' when I walked in. I watched them. It hurt me, but I got my revenge on both of them.

MARGARET. You didn't kill them?

TONY. Nah, I let her marry him. Now they're making each other miserable. I heard they're getting a divorce.

MARGARET. Maybe the both of you can work it out again.

TONY. No way. Too much water under the bridge.

MARGARET. You shouldn't say that. Sometimes things can work out. I know a couple that got a divorce and after five years got married again.

TONY. Hey, she's the one with the father, you know … I had to.

MARGARET. You're right! Too much water under the bridge. How does it feel to kill someone?

TONY. Why? You're thinking about killing someone?

MARGARET. No, I could never kill anyone.

TONY. Anybody could kill under the right conditions. Even you. Me, I kill for money. The people I kill are killers themselves. I don't wanna know nothin' about them. All I want is the name and where they live. I wait by their house. I watch every move they make. What time they leave, what time they come back.

MARGARET. Did you watch me?

TONY. Yes. I go into a trance. I get inside their heads. I picture the whole killing in my mind before it really does happen. Taking out my gun, squeezing the trigger just an eighth of an inch. I watch their life just disappear in front of me. I collect my money, and I wait for the next job. My shrink told me that … shit, that reminds me I have to call him. (*TONY walks over to the phone.*)

MARGARET. Call who?

TONY. My shrink … Oh shit, your husband's goin' to call, do you have call waiting?

MARGARET. What?

TONY. Call waiting, you know if your husband calls I'll hear it.

MARGARET. Yes, we have it.

TONY. Good, I never killed anybody before, where I had to wait for a phone call. Hey if I hear a click, does that count for one ring or two rings?

MARGARET. What are you talking about?

TONY. When I hear the click, that mean it rang once or twice? The phone when it clicks.

MARGARET. I don't know.

TONY. You got a bad attitude, baby. *(Into phone.)* Jo Jo, come on, pick up the phone.

MARGARET. *(To herself.)* Jo Jo? Your therapist's name is Jo Jo?

TONY. *(To Jo Jo.)* Jo Jo ... how ya doin'? ... Don't get mad, I took that job ... C'mon don't yell at me. Yes I know I've been making breakthroughs ... all right so this is a set back ... I have no choice, I gotta pay them back the money or I'm dead ... don't bring her up ... My sister never hurt anybody, you know what happens to me when you mention my sister's name. Just shut the fuck up about her ... JO JO please ... I'm sorry I offended you ... Please stop crying ... I didn't mean to yell at you ... look ... Just get yourself together and call me back later. The number here is 760-4542 ... wait a minute, her husband gonna call and let the phone ring twice ... When you call, you let the phone ring once, hang up and then call back so I know it's you. *(TONY hangs up.)*

MARGARET. Does your mother know what you do?

TONY. No.

MARGARET. She wouldn't like it.

TONY. My mother and father are both dead. They died in a car accident when I was ten years old.

MARGARET. You're all alone?

TONY. Everybody's alone. You die in your own arms, remember that.

MARGARET. Don't you have a sister?

TONY. Whatta you know about my sister?

MARGARET. Nothing ... I just heard you mention her that's all.

TONY. Next time you mind your fuckin' business about my sister.

MARGARET. Ok ... I'm sorry ... I was just concerned.

TONY. She was dating some young wiseguy who got outta line just like you. Certain people decided to have him killed and my sister just got in the way. It was just business.

MARGARET. They killed her, too?

TONY. Yes.

MARGARET. I'm so sorry.

MARGARET. Have you ever killed a woman ?

TONY. No. That's something I would never do.

MARGARET. Why me?

TONY. I'm in a lot of trouble. I stood up for a guy and he turned out to be a piece of shit. He stole a lot of money and now I gotta pay it back or I'm dead. Your husband paid me a lot to do this. When it's done I'll be even. I'm sorry it had to be you.

MARGARET. You're not sorry. You're a selfish bastard, just like my husband. You don't give a shit about me. All you care about is the money. You're just looking to save your own ass. Big tough guy is gonna kill a woman.

TONY. That's right. Because fifty years from now, when I'm dead and buried and someone throws that last piece of sod on my face and says "Let's break for lunch," who's really gonna give a fuck? Who really is gonna care? That's why I say get what you can get. Your husband's got the right idea. Faithful, it's all bullshit.

(The TELEPHONE rings. Both TONY and MARGARET tense. The PHONE rings the second time. TONY is ready. The PHONE rings the third time. TONY and MARGARET share a look. THEY both relax a bit. TONY walks towards the garden window and sits down for the first time.)

MARGARET. Do you think I'm pretty?
TONY. What?
MARGARET. Do you think I'm pretty?
TONY. You're all right.
MARGARET. When I was in high school, there was a girl in my class. She wasn't pretty, she was beautiful. Her hair, her eyes, her body, everything. Men just wanted to be close to her. You know why? Because she was beautiful. Every guy in school was after her. Except one. He liked me. We would go for long walks on Boston Post Road, make love in my basement, reminisce about old movies. We didn't have a dime between us but it was great. But I would watch her out of the corner of my eye and she would look at us and I could tell it bothered her because we were so happy. She always wore these tight skirts and low cut blouses. Finally one day, he called me and told me he was seeing her. It broke my heart. He said he was in

love and that she loved him too. I told him she's lying. She doesn't love you, I do. She left him a few weeks later and broke his heart. He came back to me but it was never the same. You know you'll do anything for someone you love ... except love them again.

(A long beat.)

TONY. What the fuck does that story have to do with anything? Why are you telling me this? For what? ... You're right about one thing. A man will do anything for a beautiful woman and the more beautiful the woman the more he'll do. I'm telling you, if you spoke to every con in jail right now, the reason they're behind bars, is because of a woman. Some guy killed another guy because he fucked with his woman, another guy becomes a big coke dealer so he can have all the broads he wants, a guy goes on dope because a woman left him, so now he's gotta steal. *(TONY gets up from the chair and walks over to Margaret.)* I'm telling ya, it's all because of women ... and dogs.
MARGARET. Dogs?
TONY. Yeah ... dogs, I almost killed my next door neighbor because his dog kept shitting in my yard. Dogs cause a lot of fights too.
MARGARET. So in other words, aside from dogs, anything bad that happens to a man is because of a woman.
TONY. That's right.
MARGARET. What was my mistake? I never did a damn thing wrong to my husband. I loved him more than anybody ever could.
TONY. That was your mistake, babe. You loved him too much. I'd rather be in heavy like than in love. Love has

got no middle ground. Heavy like just stays the way it is. Never gets any better, never gets any worse. It's a safer bet.

MARGARET. Isn't there any love in you?

TONY. Love is for kids.

MARGARET. Kids?

TONY. That's right ... but then they get older and they find out what the real world is all about.

MARGARET. You're wrong.

TONY. I'm wrong? Go look on death row. Everyone of those killers was a kid once.

MARGARET. What's wrong? Why do you hurt so much inside?

TONY. Don't fuck with me.

MARGARET. Talk to me, Tony. Maybe I can help you.

TONY. Help me? I'm the one with the gun. You're the one who's been good all these years, and what did you get for it? ... nothin' ... your husband's gonna get the business and a cool million. Don't you see? People don't stay together because of love. They stay together because they're scared shit of being alone.

(The PHONE starts ringing. Only ONE RING.)

TONY. As soon as your husband got some money, it gave him an extra set of balls.

(The PHONE starts to ring again.)

TONY. *(Picks it up.)* NOT NOW! ... *(HE slams the phone down.)* Why aren't you afraid?

MARGARET. Afraid of what?

TONY. Of me ... to die.

MARGARET. Look on that desk ... do you see that note? ... why don't you read it.

TONY. (*Picks up the note and starts to read it.*) "To my husband, I know that you've been unfaithful to me. I've known that for a long time now. But now I know there's someone special in your life, someone you really care about. I'm sorry that I was never able to give you children but you knew that when you married me. I can't live like this any longer ... that's why I decided to take my own life ..." (*To Margaret.*) Hey what the fuck is this? You were gonna kill yourself?

MARGARET. Do you see the bottle right on top of the desk? It's Dalmane, very fast, very painless. Just before you came into the room and tied me up. I was going to take the whole bottle, but you stopped me instead. (*Laughs.*) You saved my life, and now you're going to kill me. So that's why I'm not afraid. I was already dead before you came in. You're just doing me a favor. So why don't you just do what you have to do, big shot?

TONY. Not yet.

MARGARET. Oh that's right, you have to wait for the phone call. You're the best, right? You never make a mistake. You never go back on your word, isn't that right, Tony? Who's in the Mafia. Who's a hit man. Who never killed a woman before.

TONY. You'd better stop pushing me. I told you how you're gonna die. It's not gonna be that easy. I'm gonna tear your clothes off, and rape you ... and then I'm gonna put a bullet in the back of your head. Does that sound like fun, baby?

(The TELEPHONE rings ONCE. TONY and MARGARET tense. The ringing stops. TONY walks over to the phone and waits. It starts to RING AGAIN. TONY picks up the phone.)

TONY. What! ... YES! I KNOW IT'S YOU! ... I'm sorry I hung up on you ... no ... it's not because I think less of you ... no ... she doesn't think less of you either ... she doesn't even know you ... no ... no ... I can't ask her ... please don't cry ... all right I'll ask her. *(To Margaret.)* Maggie do you think less of my shrink because he cried?

MARGARET. No.

TONY. *(Back to Jo Jo.)* She said no ... what? ... *(To Margaret.)* He didn't hear you, could you say it again? *(This time TONY holds the phone out towards Margaret.)*

MARGARET. No.

TONY. All right! You happy now? ... SHE SAID IT ... NO I DIDN'T TELL HER TO SAY IT ... FUCK YOU ... IT DOESN'T MATTER ... SHE'S GONNA BE DEAD SOON ... GOODBYE. *(TONY hangs up the phone.)* This fuckin' Jo Jo is driving me crazy. I go to him for help and he is driving me crazy. He bought me this book for my birthday. *The Road Less Traveled* ... He told me to make sure I read the first line ... "Don't forget, read the first line." I open it up and I read the first line "Life is difficult," it said ... No shit ... I threw the fuckin' book in the garbage. Just because you write a book doesn't mean you're smart, you know ... I'm hungry ... where's the kitchen?

MARGARET. Through there.

(TONY walks off stage into the kitchen.)

TONY. (*Offstage.*) It's white.
MARGARET. What?
TONY. (*Offstage.*) The bread. It's white! This shit will kill ya ... Fuckin' people got all the money in the world ... and don't know how to eat right. Make myself a nice sandwich. Shit!
MARGARET. What?
TONY. (*Offstage.*) It's crunchy!
MARGARET. What?
TONY.(*Offstage.*) The peanut butter ... It's crunchy? I like the creamy and you got the crunchy.
MARGARET. I ...
TONY. (*Offstage.*) Peanut butter's been around a hundred years and people gotta fuck with it by puttin' crunches in it.
MARGARET. Well ...
TONY. (*Offstage.*) I'm telling ya, you people are unbelievable.

(TONY finishes making his peanut butter and jelly sandwich and comes out of the kitchen. HE turns around and sees MARGARET staring at him.)

TONY. What? ... You hungry?
MARGARET. Yes.
TONY. Here ... You can have half of my peanut butter and jelly sandwich. (*TONY places half of his sandwich on a table in front of Margaret.*)
MARGARET. How am I supposed to eat it?
TONY. That's your problem.

MARGARET. Can't you untie me?

TONY. Forget it.

MARGARET. I'm hungry.

TONY. I said, forget it … You're not going to trick me.

MARGARET. Well, if you're not going to untie me, you're going to have to feed me.

TONY. (*Looks at her in disbelief.*) What?

MARGARET. Feed me.

TONY. Feed you? Okay. You want me to feed you? All right. I'll feed you.

(*TONY looks at her for a beat then holds the sandwich out so she can take a bite. MARGARET leans forward and is about to take a bite when TONY quickly flips the sandwich upward hitting the tip of her nose, leaving a dab of peanut butter and jelly on it. TONY laughs. MARGARET starts to cry.*)

MARGARET. That was a shitty thing to do.

TONY. Hey, c'mon. It was a joke … I'm sorry.

(*TONY wipes her nose off. THEY look at each other for a moment. An awkward moment as THEY look at each other, neither one knowing what to do. Then, TONY breaks the moment as HE offers her the sandwich again. HE looks away, uncomfortable. SHE cautiously takes a bite, never taking her eyes off Tony. SHE eats. HE waits.*)

MARGARET. I just want you to know that's it's ok.

TONY. What's ok?

MARGARET. To kill me … I know that you're in a lot

of trouble and you need the money. You're just doing what you were paid to do. I just want you to know that I understand. I'm still hungry, do you mind if—

TONY. (*Offers her another bite.*) Yeah ... sure.

MARGARET. You see, Tony, you can be nice if you want too.

TONY. Yeah.

MARGARET. I bet you're really a nice guy.

TONY. (*Uncomfortable.*) I'm ok.

MARGARET. What were you like when you were a kid?

TONY. I don't remember, I haven't been a kid since I was ten years old.

MARGARET. What did you want to be?

TONY. C'mon, stop the bullshit. I know what you're trying to do.

MARGARET. No I mean it ... didn't you have any dreams?

TONY. Yeah ... I wanted to be one of the little kings.

MARGARET. Little kings?

TONY. Every Sunday my parents would take me to church and we would see all of them standing on the corner. They would tip their hats for my mother and my father would nod and politely smile at them. Everybody respected these guys. They had it all, the money, the cars, the women ... and I would say "Daddy I want to be like them, everybody treats them like kings." ... and my father told me "only in this neighborhood do the little kings mean anything, son, outside of this neighborhood they're nobodies." He was right ... I miss my father.

MARGARET. You're a good man ...

TONY. Yeah, sure ...

MARGARET. Do you like me? ... I like you ... Do you find me desirable? ... If you were my husband, would you let four months go by without making love to me? ... Would you?

TONY. No ... I wouldn't.

MARGARET. You wouldn't what?

TONY. Let four months go by.

MARGARET. Do you want to make love to me?

TONY. No ... I can't.

MARGARET. Why? ... can't get it up?

TONY. I have no problem with that.

MARGARET. Well then untie me and take me in the bedroom and do it.

TONY. I can't untie you.

MARGARET. Well then leave me tied up. It might be fun.

TONY. I can't do it.

MARGARET. Why? ... C'mon Tony, you said you have to rape me anyway, so let's at least make it fun for both of us.

TONY. That's not the way I work.

MARGARET. How do you work?

TONY. (Snapping.) That's enough!

MARGARET. My husband just does it once and then he rolls over and dies. All the lights have to be shut off and he doesn't say a word ... nothing, not even a moan. I feel like I'm making love to a dead man.

TONY. Look there's making love and then there's fucking. They are two different things. A man will say and do anything before he comes, but once he comes, he wants out. He wants to get something to eat, watch television, read a book. If he says different he's lying.

MARGARET. But he makes me feel like a hooker ... did you ever go with a hooker Tony?

TONY. I only go with hookers.

MARGARET. Why? You're not a bad looking guy.

TONY. It's easier, you give them money and they give you what you want, it cuts all the bullshit.

MARGARET. Let's just do it?

TONY. Do what?

MARGARET. Make love.

TONY. No.

MARGARET. Tony, c'mon untie me. I really can be good with the right person. When you make love do you talk?

TONY. You're really something.

MARGARET. Well I just thought if we're going to do it, we might as well get to know one another since we have a time problem here ... now do you talk?

(SHE's turning him on and HE starts to give in to the seduction.)

TONY. OK ... Yeah ... I talk.

(HE starts moving closer to her. SHE's sitting, HE's standing.)

MARGARET. Great ... I love a man who talks to me in bed. Now are you gentle or are you rough?

TONY. I'm a little bit of both.

MARGARET. Sort of a gentle rough.

TONY. That's me.

MARGARET. That's me, too. You see, we are really

communicating here. Now, do you cuddle?

TONY. Do I what?

MARGARET. Cuddle, you know, after you make love. Do you cuddle?

TONY. No. By the time a woman wants to cuddle with me, I got my key in the car door.

MARGARET. Untie me, Tony. Make love to me, let me be your hooker and I promise you don't have to cuddle. Just untie me and I'll do anything you want.

TONY. Anything I want?

MARGARET. Anything ... Come on ... untie me, Tony. Take me. Touch me. Anything you want.

(TONY gets closer and closer to her, reaches out for her face. Then suddenly HE grabs her roughly and pushes her away.)

TONY. You slut ... You shoulda been faithful. You deserve to die.

MARGARET. Don't you tell me I deserve to die because I was unfaithful. My husband's the one who wasn't faithful.

TONY. That's right and he couldn't give two shits about you, so just shut up.

MARGARET. No. I'm not going to shut up. It's not right. Just because he's a man, he gets away with it. He thinks he's going to get it all, but he's going to end up with nothing ... and so are you ... Tony, you're so stupid.

TONY. You better watch your mouth.

MARGARET. Why? What are you going to do, kill me? You're just like my husband ... stupid.

TONY. I'm warning you, stop playing with me.

MARGARET. Don't you realize what's happening here? You've been played for a fool.

TONY. What are you talking about?

MARGARET. My husband didn't hire you … I did.

TONY. Don't play with me.

MARGARET. I'm not playing, I'm serious.

TONY. Stop it!!! … you're trying to trick me.

MARGARET. Trick you? Did you meet my husband?

TONY. No.

MARGARET. Do you know what he looks like?

TONY. No.

MARGARET. Then how do you know he hired you?

TONY. A man gave me half the money up front.

MARGARET. Was it my husband?

TONY. No … but that doesn't matter.

MARGARET. Why not?

TONY. Because that's the way it's always done. The money is always given by a third party.

MARGARET. Then how do you know it was my husband and not me who hired you?

TONY. Why the fuck would you hire someone to kill you?

MARGARET. Because I don't have the guts to do it myself. Look at those monitors, I can see everything. What comes in and out of this place. Nothing gets by me. Today I saw you climb over the wall and walk towards the side window. You see, Tony, I watched you.

TONY. You're fuckin' lying.

MARGARET. I could of stopped you but I didn't. I was happy to see you. So the deal's off. Just untie me.

TONY. So help me God I'll kill you.

MARGARET. Good! I'm throwing in one hundred

thousand dollars to sweeten the pot. You're the best, right? You never go back on your word. Make him die and I want him to know that I paid you to do it.

TONY. (*Pulls out a gun and puts it to her head.*) I'm warning you, slut. You're twisting everything around. One more word and I'll ...

MARGARET. You'll what, kill me? ... No you won't. You never killed a woman before, remember? That's something you would never do!

(The Phone RINGS once.)

TONY. We'll find out right now. (*HE cocks the gun.*

(The PHONE stops.)

TONY. Shit.

(The PHONE starts to ring again.)

TONY. (*Sweeps in to pick it up.*) Jo Jo ... we got a definite problem here ... I need a session right now ... She just told me she hired me ... She knows everything ... She saw me on the monitors climb over the wall ... . She's driving me crazy ... What? ... JO JO that's not a good idea ... What's wrong with you ... I don't want to get you involved ... Don't be a fuckin' idiot ... all right ... I didn't mean to yell at you ... all right ... don't cry ... (*To Margaret.*) ... He wants to talk to you.

MARGARET. Me?

TONY. Yeah ... be nice, he's very sensitive ... (*TONY walks over and puts the phone to Margaret's ear.*)

MARGARET. Jo Jo? ... where the hell did you get your degree ... why? ... because I can't believe people go to you for help ... you're the one who needs help ... (*To Tony.*) ... he's crying ...

TONY. (*Pulls the phone away.*) Jo Jo I'm having a hard time here ... what ... stop blaming my sister ... It wasn't her fault ... she never hurt anybody ... he was a piece if shit ... I don't wanna talk to you ... 'bye. (*TONY hangs up the phone and is badly shaken. HE is losing it fast.*)

MARGARET. C'mon Tony untie me ... the deal's off.

TONY. Not yet. (*TONY picks up the bottle of pills and runs into the kitchen. HE opens up the bottle of pills and dumps them in the palm of his hand. Offstage.*) Look, you can make things easy for both of us. I mean you were gonna do it anyway. Just take the pills. It's better for everybody involved.

MARGARET. Better for everybody involved? Not for me it isn't.

TONY. (*Offstage.*) Just take the pills then I won't have to hurt you.

MARGARET. No.

TONY. (*Re-enters the living room with the pills in one hand and a glass of water in the other.*) What do you mean "no"?

MARGARET. If you want me dead, you're gonna have to do it yourself.

TONY. Take the pills.

MARGARET. Then kill my husband.

TONY. I can't do that ... that wasn't the deal ... (*TONY puts the glass of water down and starts forcing the pills in MARGARET's mouth.*) Just take the fuckin' pills. Take the pills now, I said open your mouth. Don't fight it, you were gonna do it anyway. Open your mouth, I said open it.

(SHE bites his hand. HE screams in pain and then HE slaps her. There's a long pause. TONY just stares at her. SHE spits out the few pills that he was able to get in her mouth.)

TONY. You want your husband dead, Maggie?

MARGARET. Yes.

TONY. You really want him dead?

MARGARET. Oh God, yes.

TONY. *(Pulls out the gun and places it on the table in front of Margaret.)* Then how about if I take the hundred thousand and leave you the gun. You think you could kill him? I could teach you how. Just an eighth of an inch, that's all it takes, Maggie. All you have to do is squeeze this little trigger here and no matter how much money he's got, how tough he thinks he is, no matter what he accomplished in his whole life means nothing, if you squeeze this. C'mon can you do it?

MARGARET. *(SHE thinks about it, then—) I can't.*

TONY. Yes you can Maggie, anybody can kill.

MARGARET. No.

TONY. You're telling me that you would rather die than kill him?

MARGARET. Yes.

TONY. I don't believe you. You know what your problem is? You're not mad enough.

MARGARET. Leave me alone.

TONY. Think about it, one million dollars, do you know how much fun he's gonna have with all that?

MARGARET. I can't do it.

TONY. It doesn't bother you that after you're dead he's going to be enjoying life with his new girl friend?

MARGARET. Shut up … just shut up …

TONY. He's not even going to remember you.

MARGARET. Fuck you … you bastard!!!

TONY. They gonna make babies together.

MARGARET. (*SHE breaks down and begins to cry.*) STOP IT!!! … STOP IT!!!… no more … please.

TONY. You're too pure, Maggie, my sister was pure like you, and the real world swallowed her up.

MARGARET. I know what happened to your sister.

TONY. You shut the fuck up about my sister.

MARGARET. You killed her.

TONY. You mind your fuckin' business.

MARGARET. You killed her.

TONY. I didn't do it.

MARGARET. Yes you did, you killed your own flesh and blood.

(*The phone RINGS. Once. Twice. Then stops. THEY both stare at each other.*)

TONY. It's time.

MARGARET. Tony.

TONY. You shoulda taken my offer.

MARGARET. I don't want to die.

TONY. I've got no choice. (*HE grabs her and starts untying her.*)

MARGARET. Please don't kill me. I don't want to die anymore.

(*TONY unties her from the chair, but HER hands remain*

tied behind her back. HE throws her on the couch,
forces her face into the cushion, stopping her from
screaming, and puts the gun to the back of her head.)

TONY. They're gonna kill me if I don't pay the money
back ... you don't understand, I gotta kill you ...

MARGARET. (*Twists in Tony's grip to face him.*)
Please, Tony, no ...

TONY. I'm sorry, Maggie ... I have to do this ...

MARGARET. I'll give you anything you want ... Oh
God ... please ...

TONY. Shut up ... just shut up ...

MARGARET. Tony, Tony ...

TONY. I've got no choice ... (*TONY hurls the gun*
against the wall. HE sits on the edge of the couch and
starts to cry.) I had no choice ... I warned my sister to stay
away from him but she wouldn't listen, she told me they
were in love and they were going to get married and they
were gonna live happily ever fuckin' after, just like you did
Maggie. I mean she was the only thing I had left in the
world. He knew there was a contract out on him and that's
why he kept her with him every minute of the day. He
knew I couldn't touch him with her around. So I went to
his apartment and waited in the darkness. I said a prayer to
myself that he would be alone. But as I heard the key in the
door, I heard her laugh and I realized that my prayers
weren't answered. He opened the door and I pointed my
gun at him and my sister started screaming "Please Tony,
don't kill him!" I told her to get away from him ... but he
grabbed her and he put his gun to her head ... he told me to
leave and everything would be forgotten. I told him, "Fuck
you. You're gonna die" ... It was me or him, he had to die,

so I killed him.

MARGARET. And your sister?

TONY. He deserve to die.

MARGARET. Tony …

TONY. He had no respect for anybody.

MARGARET. Tony, your sister?

TONY. I gave my word.

MARGARET. Your sister, what happened?

TONY. I killed her.

MARGARET. Why?

TONY. When I shot him, he pulled the trigger on my sister.

MARGARET. Tony, you didn't do it.

TONY. Yes I did. It's my fault. If I would have left that apartment, my sister would be alive now.

MARGARET. But you said you had no choice.

TONY. That's right, I had no choice. Just like now, I've got to kill you.

MARGARET. No, Tony. (*Soothingly.*) You could untie me and let me help you. Come on, Tony, it's gonna be all right. We've both been hurt. We can help each other. You have to forgive yourself about your sister. It wasn't your fault. Untie me, I can help you.

(*During the above, MARGARET works her way across the couch to Tony, close to him. HER voice growing more hypnotic. SHE sees the gun lying on the floor. TONY still shaken, begins to untie her.*)

MARGARET. That's it, you're a good man Tony. You didn't mean to hurt anybody. It's wasn't your fault. (*SHE's rubbing his back, wiping the tears from his eyes. SHE takes another look at the gun and then their eyes meet.)* We can do this thing together. I'll open the safe for you. I can help you. You can have all the money.

(SHE takes one more look at the gun and tries to reach it, while TONY is kissing her neck.)

BLACKOUT

ACT II

SCENE: The same. The stage is empty. We hear JACK *off stage.*

JACK. (*Offstage.*) Hello? ... Margaret? ... Margaret? (*JACK enters the living room. HE is in his mid-forties. HE just stands there for a moment, quietly. HE is carrying his briefcase and a bottle of champagne.*) Margaret? ... Margaret.

MARGARET. Jack!

(*SHE comes around the corner. JACK is noticeably startled, speechless. MARGARET is dressed beautifully. A very sexy dress. SHE seems happy, energetic.*)

MARGARET. What happened? I was getting worried.

JACK. What happened?

MARGARET. I thought something might have happened to you.

JACK. To me?

MARGARET. Yes.

JACK. A couple of trucks came in late and we just got backed up.

MARGARET. Are you okay?

JACK. I'm fine ... why?

MARGARET. You look terrible ... champagne! What are we celebrating?

JACK. What are we celebrating? Don't you

remember? It's our anniversary twenty years.

MARGARET. In two months.

JACK. What?

MARGARET. Our anniversary is two months away.

JACK. It is?

MARGARET. Yes.

JACK. I need a drink.

MARGARET. Why don't I get some glasses. (*MARGARET heads to the kitchen.*)

JACK. How come you're so dressed up?

MARGARET. (*Offstage.*) I had a great day today.

JACK. What was so great about it?

MARGARET. (*Offstage.*) I don't know. It was just one of those days when everything goes right.

JACK. Yeah, I've had some of those, but not today. Today has been a disaster.

MARGARET. (*Returns with the champagne glasses.*) To twenty years of marriage, even though it's two months early.

JACK. Anything unusual happen today?

MARGARET. No.

JACK. Just a regular day?

MARGARET. Yes ... Why?

JACK. Oh, just curious.

MARGARET. Jack.

JACK. Yes.

MARGARET. Are you ok?

JACK. Yes, I was just thinking.

MARGARET. About what?

JACK. About what? I don't know. Twenty years, seems like a lifetime ago.

MARGARET. Why do you look so sad? Did something

not work out as you planned?

JACK. No. It's nothing really, I'm just glad you're here. Twenty years, wow.

MARGARET. That's right twenty years. Do you remember the basement?

JACK. Yes.

MARGARET. We would put the mattress on the floor so my parents wouldn't hear the bed squeaking when we made love.

JACK. They knew anyway.

MARGARET. The way my father used to come down the steps, yelling my name five times before he'd walk thought the door.

JACK. Remember those long walks on Boston Post Road, with the cars beeplng their horns because your dress was so short.

MARGARET. They don't beep anymore.

JACK. C'mon, you're as beautiful as the day I met you.

MARGARET. Beautiful? You really think so?

JACK. Would I lie to you?

(A moment of tension as MARGARET does not answer but just stares at Jack. Uncomfortable, JACK rises, taking off his jacket and tie as HE moves. MARGARET follows.)

MARGARET. Did you ever go with a hooker, Jack?

JACK. What?

MARGARET. A prostitute.

JACK. Why are you asking me this?

MARGARET. Did you ever pay to have sex with another woman?

JACK. No.

MARGARET. No? Jack, I grew up in the same neighborhood as you, I knew those guys you hung out with. You're telling me never?

JACK. Ok. When I was a kid, I did it once at a bachelor party.

MARGARET. Did you like it?

JACK. I don't remember.

MARGARET. Did you ever get kinky?

JACK. What?

MARGARET. Kinky. You know with one of those hookers.

JACK. What the hell's gotten into you?

MARGARET. For the past four months nothing.

JACK. Honey I know we haven't made love in a while, I've been so busy.

(MARGARET pulls out a piece of rope from Jack's desk. It's the same rope that Tony had tied her with.)

JACK. What's that?

MARGARET. This is kinky. Let me tie you up, Jack.

JACK. What?

MARGARET. It turns me on.

JACK. Since when?

MARGARET. Today.

JACK. Today? Why?

MARGARET. You've been a bad boy.

JACK. I have? What did I do?

MARGARET. It's what you tried to do.

JACK. What did I try to do?

MARGARET. Oh ... you know, Jack.

JACK. No. I don't know.

MARGARET. Jack, let's do it.

JACK. Do what?

MARGARET. Right here on the floor. (*SHE gets down on the floor and tries to pull HIM down.*)

JACK. Do what on the floor?

MARGARET. I want to make love to my husband.

JACK. On the floor?

MARGARET. Yes.

JACK. I can't.

MARGARET. Don't I turn you on?

JACK. Margaret! ... please.

MARGARET. Do me right here on the floor.

JACK. Margaret, have you been taking your medication?

MARGARET. Do you want to fuck your wife or not?

JACK. You need to see your shrink.

(*JACK pushes her away. The PHONE rings once. MARGARET goes to answer it but it has stopped ringing.*)

JACK. (*Referring to her behavior.*) What the hell is going on here?

MARGARET. What?

(*The PHONE starts to ring again.*)

MARGARET. (*Picks it up.*) I'll get it. (*Into phone.*) Hello ... hi ... no ... not now ... no ... I don't think less of you ... My father gambled, it didn't make him a bad person ... Thank you anyway but I have a therapist ...

Don't cry … Look, I've got to go … 'Bye. (*SHE hangs up.*)

JACK. Who was that?

MARGARET. Who was what?

JACK. On the phone.

MARGARET. A therapist.

JACK. You already have a therapist.

MARGARET. Yeah, I know. Linda Fisher recommended him to me. She said he was very good. She thinks after five years maybe it's time for a change. She came over for lunch yesterday. She's very upset. She thinks Bob is cheating on her.

JACK. Really? What makes her think that?

MARGARET. A woman knows.

JACK. What do you mean "a woman knows"?

MARGARET. She said Bob doesn't touch her the same.

JACK. Come on, they're married fifteen years, that happens.

MARGARET. I saw Bob with another woman.

JACK. When?

MARGARET. What's the difference?

JACK. Maybe it was just a friend.

MARGARET. They were holding hands across a candle-lit table.

JACK. Did you tell Linda?

MARGARET. Should I have?

JACK. Of course not.

MARGARET. Oh really, why?

JACK. It's better to mind your own business.

MARGARET. Why do men cheat, Jack?

JACK. Let's not get into that now.

MARGARET. Linda is a beautiful woman. They have everything. Is it because she's getting old?

JACK. It's in the genes, some men just have to do it, that's all.

MARGARET. What? Fuck?

JACK. Margaret.

MARGARET. Do they have to fuck every woman they see?

JACK. It's the action.

MARGARET. What are you talking about?

JACK. Men who like the action don't care if they sleep with the woman or not. It's like being a degenerate gambler. You don't really care if you win or lose. It's the action.

MARGARET. Can't one woman make a man happy?

JACK. Yes ... the one he can't have. I'm not talking about me, it's just that a lot of other men feel that way.

MARGARET. Are you happy, Jack?

JACK. Me? ... Yes ... very happy, why all the questions?

MARGARET. I don't know. I mean look at Bob, he has everything and he still cheats.

JACK. Margaret, don't compare me to him. Some men are just weak, that's all.

MARGARET. Linda knows, Jack.

JACK. Knows what?

MARGARET. That Bob is cheating on her.

JACK. You told her?

MARGARET. No.

JACK. Don't bullshit me Margaret. Bob is a good friend of mine. Did you tell her?

MARGARET. I said no, and what do you mean Bob is

a good friend of yours? Linda is being stepped on and all you care about is your friend?

JACK. I know you told her.

MARGARET. I didn't tell her, but I wish I did. She spent the whole lunch crying. She felt like her life was shattered. All because your "good friend, Bob" told her he was in love with another woman.

JACK. Maybe they just grew apart.

MARGARET. Bullshit Jack, he's just a selfish bastard, and you know what really hurts? She never knew. She didn't even have a clue. He was the perfect husband, taking the kids to school, coaching the little league team, he was a real low life.

JACK. Bob's a good man, Margaret. He's just got his problems like anybody else. He told me he just fell out of love with Linda. Besides, he met someone he really cares about.

MARGARET. Oh really, who? Do I know her?

JACK. No, I met her, she's a great girl.

MARGARET. How old is she?

JACK. Twenty-four, but I know you, don't jump to conclusions. Bob does not support her, she takes care of herself.

MARGARET. What does she do?

JACK. She's a cocktail waitress.

MARGARET. Is it possible for a man to be faithful today?

JACK. Why is it always the man … women cheat too Margaret, maybe someday you'll be unfaithful to me. All I know is that Bob told me he was faithful to Linda for fifteen years, that's got to count for something.

MARGARET. Count for what? He built up enough

good points so now he can cheat? Just because he put fifteen good years into a marriage, it does not give him the right to be unfaithful.

JACK. You have no idea what pressure Bob was under.

MARGARET. What pressures? What? Mid-life crisis? That excuse for a man to act like a child again?

JACK. It's so easy for you, isn't it. You sit on your ass all damn day and watch those monitors and at night you take your pill and go to sleep. Bob had to go out in the world and be a success. Women can always marry success, men can't. Women are born with a parachute on their back. When life gets too hard, all they have to do is pull the ripcord and get married.

MARGARET. That's bullshit and you know it.

JACK. No it's not. In the eyes of the world a woman can never be a failure. The worst they can be is a housewife.

MARGARET. I'm a housewife, Jack, is that the worst thing I could be?

JACK. Margaret, listen ...

MARGARET. No ... you listen Mr. Success. When my father died and left *me* the house, it was *my* idea to sell it and use the money to start our own business.

JACK. Don't you throw that up in my face.

MARGARET. When we got married we had nothing. Where was my "parachute" then? Don't think I'm a fool, Jack, I know what's going on.

JACK. What are you talking about?

MARGARET. You've been seeing other women. I've known that for years, I dealt with that, but what really hurts me is now I know there's someone you care about and you're not even man enough to admit it.

JACK. Margaret that's not true. I ...

MARGARET. Don't lie to me Jack. Do you think I'm really that stupid? I found out about your five day excursion to Puerto Rico. The travel agent called me to confirm the reservations. The credit card receipts from restaurants that you never took me to. I know all about you little personal assistant Debbie.

JACK. Debbie? Debbie works for me.

MARGARET. No. Debbie works on you.

JACK. That's enough.

MARGARET. Do you thinks she loves you?

JACK. You're losing it. You need to see your shrink, fast.

MARGARET. I don't need my shrink, Mr. ... Success ... I'm going to take you to the cleaners ... I know what you re trying to do.

JACK. What? ... What did I try to do?

MARGARET. You know that the business is in my name ... and if we divorce you get nothing.

JACK. You're not divorcing me.

MARGARET. I met you with nothing, and I'm leaving you with Debbie and the fake tits.

JACK. First of all, they are not fake.

MARGARET. Just admit that I'm right.

JACK. Her tits are not fake.

MARGARET. Don't you get smart with me.

JACK. Where are your pills?

MARGARET. Just admit that you've been cheating on me all these years and you love Debbie.

JACK. Margaret, I do love you.

MARGARET. Be a man and answer the question.

JACK. It's our anniversary. Why are you doing this?

MARGARET. Our anniversary? That's a good point. I would like to know what the hell has been going on for the past twenty years. What kind of marriage is this?

JACK. Calm down. Why don't you take one of your pills. It will help you relax. I'll get it for you.

MARGARET. I don't want any pills. I want some answers.

JACK. What? What answers do you want?

MARGARET. I want to hear it from your lips, have you been faithful to me?

JACK. NO.

MARGARET. Good ... that's a start ... now tell me why?

JACK. I don't know.

MARGARET. That's not good enough, I deserve an answer. When was the last time we made love?

JACK. I don't know ... I don't remember.

MARGARET. You don't remember? Let me refresh your memory, It was four months ago.

JACK. Honey, I work hard all day. I come home and I'm very tired. You've taken your pill and you're sound asleep.

MARGARET. You're lying again, Jack ... you just admitted that you've been unfaithful to me ... now ... do you love her?

JACK. No.

MARGARET. Jack, if you ever had to tell the truth in you life, you better do it now ... C'mon honey just say it. I won't be upset, do you love Debbie?

JACK. Yes.

MARGARET. You piece of shit.

JACK. Margaret!!

MARGARET. You fucking low life.

JACK. Don't you talk to me like that.

MARGARET. I made you what you are and I can break you. Do you think I'm going to roll over and die, so that you and Debbie can enjoy life? I am leaving you with nothing.

JACK. You are not leaving me. You're my wife.

MARGARET. You don't need me, you have your new love.

JACK. It's just a phase I'm going though.

MARGARET. A phase? Do you think she loves you?

JACK. Margaret … please …

MARGARET. Answer me. Do you think she loves you?

JACK. Yes.

MARGARET. Have you looked in the mirror lately?

JACK. What?

MARGARET. There's a mirror right over there. Go look in it.

JACK. Fuck you.

MARGARET. C'mon, Jack, wake up and smell the coffee. If you didn't have money, you would be carrying Debbie's bags three steps behind her at some airport. Where was Debbie twenty years ago when you were broke?

JACK. But I am not broke anymore!!

MARGARET. You will be.

JACK. I'm getting your pills.

MARGARET. I don't want anymore pills!

JACK. Margaret … I'm warning you …

(MARGARET starts pushing him, hard.

JACK is thrown off balance.)

MARGARET. What are you going to do, hit me ...
c'mon, you can't hurt me anymore.

JACK. Stop it ... Margaret!

MARGARET. Why? ... Why did you do this to me? ...
I hate you ... you took my life.

JACK. Stop it ... What the hell is wrong with you?

(THEY are struggling with each other.)

MARGARET. I made you what you are ...

JACK. Margaret ... stop it ...

MARGARET. It was my money ... you hear me ... my
money.

(JACK throws HER down on the couch.)

JACK. Calm down ... What the hell has gotten into you
today? How many times are you going to throw that
money up in my face. Okay, it is true that it was your
money that got us started. But I'm the one who's been
running the business for the past fifteen years. Let's not
forget we started out with just two trucks, we now have
fifty. We are one of the biggest independent trucking
companies in New York.

MARGARET. Please Jack, don't give me a sales pitch.

JACK. I made it what it is ... ME ... NOT YOU ... I
brought this business up from nothing, while you stayed in
the house all day and stared at those fuckin' monitors ...
but you want to know the crazy part of it ... inside I still
felt like a failure. Because I knew in my heart, if it wasn't

for you, I never would have had a shot. You were always there to remind me where I came from and I wanted to forget. Some men stick a needle in their arm, some do it with booze. I did it by seeing other women, it helped the pain go away. They didn't know the old Jack, all they saw was the success. It made me feel good. I had the clothes, the cars, the money. I wasn't a nobody anymore. When I came to work I was king.

MARGARET. You're just a little king.

JACK. A what?

MARGARET. Can't you cry, Jack?

JACK. What are you talking about?

MARGARET. I never saw you cry.

JACK. What does that have to do with anything?

MARGARET. Do you feel things like normal people do?

JACK. Of course I do.

MARGARET. I'm not sure if you do.

JACK. What are you getting at?

MARGARET. Do you have any idea how I've been feeling, or do you even care?

JACK. You're my wife, I care.

MARGARET. Your wife? ... You don't treat me like one.

JACK. I take care of you, don't I?

MARGARET. You take care of me? I'm a grown woman. Do you know what it's like to feel worthless? Maybe you don't.

JACK. I know what it's like, we didn't have two nickels too rub together when we got married ... driving that shit car, I would park a block away when we visited someone ... all our friends had new cars ... and homes ...

money in the bank ... I had a shit job, taking orders from a guy who didn't know his ass from his elbow. Do you know what it feels like when you know you can be somebody if you only had a shot ... I had greatness inside of me but I was the only one who knew it.

MARGARET. I knew it, Jack ... that's why I married you.

JACK. I was grateful for what you did, but at the same time I hated you.

MARGARET. You hated me? ... Was it because of the money?

JACK. That's part of it.

MARGARET. Did you hate me because I couldn't give you children?

JACK. That's part of it, too.

MARGARET. That's why you want to hurt me?

JACK. You know what you did, I don't have to tell you.

MARGARET. What? What did I do?

JACK. It's not worth mentioning.

MARGARET. No. Tell me. What?

JACK. You cheated on me! Admit it. I put you in a castle on a hill, anything you wanted was yours. All you had to do was ask. I pay for your shrink don't I ... Do you have any idea how much that costs me. Look at this place I bought for you. Go look in your closet and see all those clothes, the jewelry and furs ... I gave you everything.

MARGARET. I can't put everything under the sheets at night ... You kept me in this house like I was your trophy and every once in a while you would dust me off.

JACK. Did you fuck him?

MARGARET. What about Debbie?

JACK. Did you fuck him?

MARGARET. You cheated on me all your life, I do it once and I'm a whore?

JACK. I knew it, I knew you fucked him. What's the difference if it's once or a hundred times. If I asked you right now, have you been faithful to me? Your answer wouldn't be any different than mine. Besides it was more than once, wasn't it, Margaret?

MARGARET. No.

JACK. Don't lie to me.

MARGARET. We went out maybe four or five times but we only made love once.

JACK. Was it just for sex?

MARGARET. Sometimes we would just hold each other.

JACK. How romantic.

MARGARET. I needed someone to make me feel like I was alive again.

JACK. Well did he do that?

MARGARET. It was temporary.

JACK. When it was over it made you feel worse didn't it?

MARGARET. Yes.

JACK. And that's why you've been wanting to kill yourself?

MARGARET. I felt dirty.

JACK. You mean your lover is not gonna come here and rescue you?

MARGARET. No. He doesn't love me.

JACK. Do you love him?

MARGARET. I don't know what love is anymore.

JACK. I wouldn't worry about that. He's not bringing

much to the table anyway. He's just a working stiff who lives in a dump and drives a shit car.

MARGARET. What?

JACK. You had to go back to the old neighborhood to find somebody, you had to rub it in my face.

MARGARET. Did you follow me?

JACK. People talked about you, you made me look bad.

MARGARET. Jack, did you follow me?

JACK. Of course not, I hired someone to watch you.

MARGARET. You what ...?

JACK. I hired someone ... He's been watching you.

MARGARET. Who? ... What does he look like?

JACK. It doesn't matter, what's done is done.

MARGARET. What's his name?

JACK. I said it doesn't matter ... I just want you to know I forgive you and I'm willing to take you back.

MARGARET. Take me back? You're willing to forgive me?

JACK. Take a pill Margaret ...

MARGARET. No more pills, Jack ... I know everything Jack.

JACK. Know what?

MARGARET. Everything ... now I want the truth. Tell me why you were so surprised when you walk in the door tonight?

JACK. What?

MARGARET. The look on your face, you couldn't even speak.

JACK. I don't know what you're talking about.

MARGARET. Yes you do ...

JACK. You know?

MARGARET. Yes.

JACK. I didn't want to hurt you.

MARGARET. Hurt me? ... How? ... the truth, Jack.

JACK. When I came home tonight I was very scared, Debbie left the office early and said she was coming here to see you. I tried to stop her but she was crying and I just couldn't control her. I've been telling her that I was going to leave you but she just got tired of waiting. She was going to tell you everything. That's why I acted the way I did when I came in.

MARGARET. Is that the only reason?

JACK. Yes ... What other reason would there be?

MARGARET. Do you love me?

JACK. Of course I do.

MARGARET. Then how could you want to hurt me?

JACK. I'm sorry about Debbie.

MARGARET. Not Debbie, I mean really hurt me.

JACK. What are you saying?

MARGARET. I was the only one who believe in you ... I'm your wife ... we were married before God.

JACK. I don't understand what you're saying.

MARGARET. Jack ... Did you hire a man to kill me?

JACK. What!

MARGARET. Did you hire a man to kill me?

JACK. No ... of course not, I hired someone to watch you.

MARGARET. No more lies.

JACK. Margaret, what hell are you saying?

MARGARET. Please ... no more lies ...

JACK. You're my wife ... I would never hurt you ...

MARGARET. Jack, I need the truth ...

JACK. I'm telling you the truth.

MARGARET. NO YOU'RE NOT! (*Goes over to the*

desk and pull out a gun.)

JACK. What the hell are you doing? ... Where did you get that?

MARGARET. A friend, or should I say your friend.

JACK. My friend? I don't know what you're talking about.

MARGARET. Yes you do.

JACK. Put the gun down.

MARGARET. He made the same mistake you did Jack, he thought with that thing between his legs ... You're gonna end up just like him ... dead.

JACK. You killed a man? Who? What the hell is wrong with you?

MARGARET. Admit that you hired him to kill me.

JACK. Margaret you need help. Let me help you.

MARGARET. Go in the bedroom. Move.

JACK. I'm not moving.

MARGARET. Then I'll kill you right here.

JACK. You better get a hold of yourself. Who the hell do you think has been taking care of you for the past twenty years. You've got nobody, Margaret, you got nobody but me.

TONY. (*Enters from the bedroom.*) She's got me, Jack.

JACK. Who are you?

TONY. You shoulda been faithful

JACK. What the hell is going on here?

TONY. You weren't faithful.

MARGARET. This is my friend, Tony.

JACK. Are you leaving me for another man?

TONY. This guy is very good.

MARGARET. You see what I mean, Tony? He'll never admit it.

JACK. Admit what? I find another man in my home with my wife, how do you think I feel? Aren't I entitled to an explanation?

MARGARET. Look who wants an explanation.

TONY. He's very good.

JACK. (*To Tony.*) If you're not out of my house in ten seconds, I'm throwing you out.

TONY. Jack, there are people in this life you can fuck with and some you can't. I'm the can't. Why don't you take a seat. Give me the gun Maggie.

(TONY takes the gun from Margaret, then pushes JACK down on the couch.)

JACK. Margaret, what's happening here?

MARGARET. Did you hire this man to kill me?

JACK. Oh my God, no. I would never …

MARGARET. Oh yes you did.

JACK. Margaret, I've never seen this man before in my life.

TONY. You cheap bastard. You offered me only twenty-five thousand and you got hundreds of thousands in a safe.

JACK. Margaret, you told him about the safe? He wants our money, he's a thief.

MARGARET. Never mind the money. Did you hire this man to kill me?

TONY. What's so important about him admitting it? I told you he did.

MARGARET. Because I want to hear it from his lips.

TONY. You heard it from my lips.

MARGARET. That's not enough, I want him to admit

everything.

JACK. I swear on my life, I don't know him. Why did you tell him about the safe?

TONY. Hey, admit it and be a man.

JACK. For God's sake, do you mean to tell me you believe a man who comes into our house with a gun? I'm trying to save your life.

MARGARET. (*To Jack.*) He told me you gave him money, is that true, Jack?

JACK. When? Where? You've met me before?

TONY. No. I never met you.

JACK. Margaret, call the police.

TONY. You gave it to someone to give to me.

JACK. Who? What's his name?

TONY. I don't give names.

JACK. He's a fake.

MARGARET. (*To Tony.*) Who gave you the money?

TONY. I said I don't give names.

MARGARET. Why not?

TONY. Because I said so.

MARGARET. Tony are you telling me the truth?

TONY. You'll have to take my word for it.

MARGARET. I don't.

TONY. Ok, you want it this way … all right scumbag admit to your wife that you hired me.

JACK. No … that's a lie …

TONY. Say it … tell her ...

JACK. NO … I didn't do anything … I would never.

TONY. C'mon talk.

JACK. He's lying.

TONY. You're fuckin' dead, Jack. (*Puts the gun to Jack's head.*)

JACK. I swear to god it's not true ... Margaret, help me.

TONY. Fuck you, talk. You hear me.

JACK. Margaret ... please ... help me.

MARGARET. Stop it ... stop it ... Leave him alone ...

TONY. What the hell is wrong with you? We had a deal. Do you want him dead. Yes or no?

MARGARET. No!

(TONY gives Margaret a look, then with disgust throws JACK back on the couch. MARGARET runs to Jack, putting her arms around him.)

JACK. *(To Margaret.)* I knew you would never hurt me.

MARGARET. You hurt me bad, Jack.

JACK. I know, I'm sorry about Debbie.

TONY. The way I feel right now, I wanna kill both of you for nothing. You two deserve each other. All right you want your husband alive? Then I want my money.

(TONY pushes MARGARET towards the safe, then forces JACK to his knees and puts the gun to the back of his head.)

MARGARET. I don't know if I remember the combination.

TONY. Well you better remember because I'm gonna put a bullet in your husband's head.

JACK. Don't kill me ...

TONY. Open it.

MARGARET. *(Tries to open the safe but can't.)* I'm

doing it ... it won't open.

JACK. Please don't ... hurt me.

TONY. I said open it.

MARGARET. I'm doing it right, damn it. I don't understand.

TONY. Stop the bullshit. Now I want the fuckin' money or he's dead.

MARGARET. It won't open.

TONY. Say goodbye, Jack. (*Cocks the gun.*)

JACK. Don't ... please ... don't ...

MARGARET. It won't open ...

JACK. I CHANGED THE COMBINATION!!!

MARGARET. You what?

JACK. I ... ah ... I changed the combination.

MARGARET. Why?

TONY. This I wanna hear.

JACK. Honey you haven't been yourself lately. I was afraid you might do something stupid.

MARGARET. Like what?

TONY. Yeah, like what?

JACK. Honey listen ...

MARGARET. Don't honey me.

TONY. Don't honey her.

MARGARET. Why did you change the combination?

JACK. I was afraid.

MARGARET. Afraid of what?

JACK. That you'd wake up one day and take all the money and leave me.

TONY. Wait a minute ... that's a two part answer ... Were you afraid that she would leave you? ... or take all the money?

MARGARET. Good question ... thank you.

TONY. You're welcome.

MARGARET. Well, Jack ... what's your answer?

JACK. I don't know what to say.

MARGARET. I guess you just said it.

TONY. Then you Jack ... open it. (*TONY pushes JACK towards the safe.*)

MARGARET. You've been lying to me all along.

JACK. Margaret I tried ...

TONY. The safe, Jack ... open it. (*TONY pushes Jack's face up against the wall safe and puts the gun to his head.*)

JACK. I'm not giving you any money.

TONY. Then I guess you're gonna die.

JACK. You can't kill me Tony. I'm the only one who can open the safe. I'm going to teach you something about business Margaret. Tony, you want the hundred thousand dollars?

TONY. Yes.

JACK. Then you kill her.

MARGARET. Tony, we have a deal ...

TONY. So help me God I'll kill you, Jack. Now open the safe.

JACK. C'mon Tony, you're going to kill me and end up with nothing?

MARGARET. Tony the deal ...

TONY. Open it!

JACK. One hundred thousand dollars Tony, it's all yours. It's all kick back money. I can't even go to the police if I wanted to.

MARGARET. Tony, don't listen to him ...

JACK. You're a business man just like me.

MARGARET. You said you would help me Tony. You promised me.

JACK. He promised you? What's a promise to men like us? We are talking about a hundred thousand dollars here.

(There is a moment of silence. TONY turns and points the gun at Margaret.)

TONY. I'm sorry, Maggie ... I'm in too deep.

MARGARET. How could you do this to me, we have a deal.

JACK. Not here, take her in the bedroom.

TONY. I'm in too deep, let's go. *(TONY grabs her.)*

MARGARET. *(To Tony.)* You gave me your word.

JACK. I don't want to see this.

TONY. Get my money ready.

MARGARET. Let go of me.

JACK. I really didn't want to put myself through this.

MARGARET. You're just a piece of shit. I hate you, I hope you burn in hell.

(As TONY drags the kicking and fighting MARGARET towards the bedroom.)

JACK. You should of been faithful.

MARGARET. We had a deal! You lied to me! We had a deal!

TONY. *(Slaps one hand over her mouth.)* The deal's off!

(JACK is at the safe. Listening to the disappearing voices of TONY and MARGARET. Then after a few seconds of silence, a loud GUNSHOT. JACK's head drops in a moment of remorse. TONY comes out of the bedroom.

HE is putting on his jacket, with the gun in his hand.)

TONY. She's dead. (*Beat.*)

JACK. You didn't fuck her.

TONY. What?

JACK. You know the plan. It's got to look like a rape and a murder.

TONY. So you are the one.

JACK. Are you going to fuck her or not?

TONY. I am not fuckin' her … now just give me my money … now.

JACK. Take it easy, Tony … you're very emotional!

TONY. Fuck you … just pay me.

JACK. All right, I'm gonna let you off the hook, you don't have to fuck her. (*Begins to open the safe.*) It's all kick back … one hundred thousand … but that's ok … so it cost me more. (*The safe opens. JACK takes the money out of the safe and brinsg it over to the table by the couch and sits.*) You know I really shouldn't pay you. I mean you and my wife were trying to kill me. She offered to give you more money and you almost fuck up this whole deal, all because of greed.

TONY. You're calling me greedy?

JACK. (*Counting the money.*) Yes … I went to a lot of precautions in trying to find the right man to do this. They said you were a man of your word, but they forgot to tell me you were greedy.

TONY. It wasn't the money.

JACK. Oh no, was it love? C'mon, Tony, tell me? Did you fall for her? What was it?

TONY. Did you know your wife was gonna kill herself before I got here tonight. I saved her life.

JACK. Did she tell you that?

TONY. Yes.

JACK. I was afraid of that.

TONY. Of what?

JACK. Afraid she might do it. She's been wanting to kill herself for months now. That's why I hired you to kill her, you just saved me a million dollars. I couldn't afford to have her kill herself.

TONY. You're really a piece of shit.

JACK. Am I? Look who's calling me a piece of shit, a hired killer.

TONY. I'm not a hired killer, Jack.

JACK. You never killed before?

TONY. Oh no I've killed once before … I killed a piece of shit, just like you.

JACK. And you just killed again.

TONY. How do you know she's dead?

JACK. I heard the shot.

TONY. Why don't you go in the bedroom and make sure. A hundred thousand dollars, that's a lot of money, Jack. What's a matter, Jack? Got no guts? Afraid to get up close. Men like us we're not afraid of nothin', right?

JACK. I'm not like you.

TONY. That's right, Jack, you're not like me. You never kept your word in your life. You suck the life out of everything that comes near you.

JACK. Who are you to judge me?

TONY. I'm the man with the gun … and the one with the gun makes the rules. You had a gun to your wife's head all her life.

JACK. She put it in my hand.

TONY. Maybe she did, but now it's time to put it in her

hand ... Maggie!

MARGARET. (*Appears in the doorway.*) What's a matter, honey, you're not happy to see me?

JACK. (*To Tony.*) You son of a bitch.

TONY. Take it easy, Jack, you're very emotional.

JACK. You knew all along I changed the combination.

MARGARET. I tried to open the safe before you got home, that's when I knew he was telling me the truth. (*To Tony.*) You scared me.

TONY. Sorry.

MARGARET. (*To Tony.*) You're very good.

TONY. (*To Margaret.*) Thanks ... so are you.

JACK. Well what's the deal?

TONY. The deal?

JACK. What are two going to do? Kill me?

(The PHONE starts ringing. Once.
Twice.)

TONY. Kill you? That sounds like a good idea ... Let me tell you what you deserve ... (*TONY hesitates because he realizes the phone stopped after two rings. Then he begins again—*) You're nothing but a low life ...

(The PHONE starts to ring again. TONY stops. ALL
THREE look at each other. TONY nods to Margaret to
answer it. SHE picks up the phone.)

MARGARET. Hello ... Once!!! ... Let the phone ring once then call back so we know it's you. (*SHE slams the phone down.*) This is the guy you go to for help?

TONY. I know ... whatta ya want me to do?

JACK. Who was that?

TONY. Shut up and sit down.

JACK. What did you do to her?

TONY. (*Crosses over to the money and starts filling his pockets.*) I woke her up, it's over Jack. You're back where you started from, with nothing. Wait a minute, I was wrong, you still got Debbie.

MARGARET. And the fake tits.

JACK. (*To himself.*) They're not fake.

MARGARET. Give me the gun.

TONY. What?

(TONY hands the gun to MARGARET, then looks at her as SHE nervously points the gun at Jack.)

MARGARET. There's not going to be a divorce.

TONY. Take it easy, Maggie.

MARGARET. Shut up. I know what I'm doing.

TONY. (*To Margaret.*) I don't think so.

MARGARET. Just go, Tony. You have the money. You got what you want, just go. Everything's going to be al right.

TONY. It doesn't have to end this way.

MARGARET. Yes it does.

TONY. I can't let you do this. (*TONY moves between Jack and Margaret.*)

MARGARET. NO! ... get away from me.

JACK. Oh God ... thank you, Tony ... thank you ...

TONY. You don't deserve it ,but I'm gonna do you a favor Jack.

JACK. Thank you ... oh God ... thank you ...

TONY. (*To Margaret.*) You never killed anybody

before.

MARGARET. So what.

JACK. Listen to him.

TONY. (*Turns and looks at Jack. To Margaret.*) Shoot him in the back of the head he'll die faster … (*TONY starts to leave. HE stops and looks back at MARGARET who still has the gun trained on Jack.*)   You take care of yourself, Maggie.

(*MARGARET gives Tony a nervous half smile and then looks back at Jack. TONY looks to Jack. TONY disappears down the hallway. There's a long silence, as MARGARET and JACK just stare at each other. THEY hear the front DOOR open and close.*)

JACK. Put the gun down, Margaret. I'm your husband, you're not going to kill me. I know Tony talked you into this, he's very good, now put the gun down.

(*MARGARET tightens her grip.*)

JACK. What are you gonna gain out of this, Margaret? I'm gonna be dead and you're gonna spend the rest of your life in jail. I'm sorry about what I did. If you want to talk about it, we can … but you have to put the gun down.

(*SHE puts the gun down on the coffee table.*)

JACK. Your shrink told me you're a very sick woman, you need help. Let me take care of you …

MARGARET. My shrink lined it all up for me but I never had the guts to make a move. He told me there's this thing called fusion where two people lock into each other. They stay in an infantile state, a symbiosis of feeding off each other; it's a sickness. They never grow up and they never really commit to each other, that's us, Jack.

JACK. Is that what I pay your shrink for? To fill your head with a bunch of shit?

MARGARET. You don't have a clue to what I'm feeling inside, do you? Do you think I'm going to forget what happened here today and just go back to playing house?

JACK. You got no choice ... you can't make it on your own, you know that. Who's going to run the business? You need me and I need a drink. Do you want to get me a drink? ... or should I get it myself?...

(JACK watches Margaret. SHE does not move.)

JACK. I'll get it myself. (*Goes to get a drink.*)

MARGARET. Big tough guy had to hire somebody to kill his wife, what's a matter you couldn't do it yourself? ... afraid to get up close?

JACK. Margaret, please, you're starting to sound like that greaseball.

MARGARET. You're a coward, Jack ... how does it feel to be a coward?

JACK. I think you better go to bed.

MARGARET. Does Debbie know that you're a coward? Maybe I should tell her.

JACK. That's enough!

MARGARET. Enough? ... Are you getting tough with me? Pick up the gun if you're so tough.

JACK. (*Looking at the gun.*) Don't tempt me.

MARGARET. C'mon big shot, it's right there. Do you think that Debbie was going to make you happy? No, but there will always be another Debbie with you Jack, you'll always find that one person that gets impressed by your bullshit and after the high is over you'll find another. You're not capable of being faithful to one woman ... You know why? ... Because all you want out of life is pleasure ... Happiness is something that's gotta be earned.

JACK. There goes that fuckin' shrink again.

MARGARET. I'm going to hurt you Jack. I'm going to hurt you bad, not in the heart ... but in the pocket ... because that's the only place where you'll feel it. I am leaving with nothing. This marriage is finished, now I want you out of this house.

JACK. What?

MARGARET. Get the fuck out of this house now!

JACK. You better take it easy baby, you don't have your knight in shining armor around any more, you better think about that.

MARGARET. (*Picks up the gun and puts it in her purse.*) OK ... but sooner or later you have to fall asleep ... you better think about that.

(THEY both stare at each other—it's a stand off. JACK looks in Margaret's eyes and sees that she means it ... HE backs down for the first time in their marriage. HE moves to get his jacket and tie.)

JACK. Okay. I hope you realize what you're doing. What are you gonna do? Go back to the working stiff? It's cold out there. Go ahead. See what's out there. Nobody's gonna want you, a woman your age, the best years behind her, couldn't give a man a child.

MARGARET. Jack, please ... that game is over.

JACK. (*Walks towards the front door.*) You're making a big mistake.

MARGARET. I don't think so.

JACK. You know ... I'll survive.

MARGARET. So will I.

(HE exits out the front door. We hear the sound of Jack's CAR pulling away. MARGARET slips into a chair. SHE sits alone in the living room, for the first time SHE hears the silence ... it feels good ... There's a TAPPING on the window that startles her. SHE sees the image of a MAN through the window in the garden. It is TONY. HE comes in though the garden doors.)

MARGARET. What are you doing here? I thought you left.

TONY. I just thought I'd hang around awhile in case you might need me.

MARGARET. You heard everything?

TONY. Yeah ... "Sooner or later you'll have to fall asleep" ... that was good ... that was very good.

MARGARET. Yeah.

TONY. Whatta you gonna do now?

MARGARET. I don't know ... find myself a lawyer and try to get my life together.

TONY. That's good.

MARGARET. Why? ... You care?

TONY. Yeah ... I care.

MARGARET. What about you?

TONY. I'm gonna pay these guys back the money I

owe them ... and then ... who knows.

MARGARET. That's good.

TONY. (*Trying to find the words.*) You know ... what happened between us ...

MARGARET. In the bedroom?

TONY. Yes.

MARGARET. Yes?

TONY. It's been a long time since I've been with a woman like that.

MARGARET. (*With a smile.*) And it was free.

TONY. Yeah it was. It was ... ah ... nice.

MARGARET. Yes it was ... thanks.

TONY. For what?

MARGARET. I don't know ... but I feel different.

TONY. Me too. I better go.

MARGARET. Yeah.

TONY. Take care of yourself.

MARGARET. You too.

TONY. (*Starts to walk towards the door. After a few steps HE turns and looks back at her.*) You know, maybe when things settle down, you and I can go out and have a cup of coffee or something?

MARGARET. Maybe. When things settle down.

TONY. (*Walks towards the front door, stops and turns—*) You know, Maggie, if you were a guy I wouldn't mind hanging out with you.

(*THEY share a smile. TONY turns and walks out the door.
(MARGARET watches him shut the door. SHE leans back in her chair and runs her fingers through her hair. After a moment SHE walks over to the monitors and shuts them off.*)

BLACKOUT
END OF PLAY

COSTUMES

MAGGIE—ACT I

Well-worn jeans

Man's blue and white striped unstarched shirt, sleeves
rolled up.

Wide gold wedding band with large simulated diamond.

Hair simple pulled-back style, slightly messed.

Minimal make-up

Bare-foot

MAGGIE—ACT II

Dark blue designer suit with gold button.

Gold lame jewel-necked top.

Dark blue high heels with gold stud trim.

Nylons

Large gold hoop earrings with pearl drop.

Wide gold wedding band with large simulated diamond.

Full make-up

Well coifed

TONY—ACT I

White shirt

Dark sports jacket

Black pants

Black shoes

Black socks

Thin black leather gloves

TONY—ACT II

Same as Act I. Except sports jacket is in the bedroom and
shirt sleeves are rolled up.

JACK—ACT II
Dark gray-blue suit
Light gray tie with blue markings
Light blue shirt
Dark blue socks
Black shoes

PROPERTY PLOT

Couch
Chair
Cigarette lighter
Desk chair on wheels
Pillow under coffee table
On desk:
    Phone
    Letter opener
    Papers
    Suicide note
    Pills
    Purse
Side board:
    Rope
    Towel
    Napkins
    Glasses
    Coasters
    Booze
    Keys
Champagne glasses
Money roll (in safe)
Two Collins glasses w/water
Peanut butter & jelly sandwich in bag
Slice of white bread
Shake can
Briefcase (Jack)
Gun, handkerchief, gloves (Tony)

FAITHFUL - Chazz Palminteri (top), Bridget Hanley, James Handy

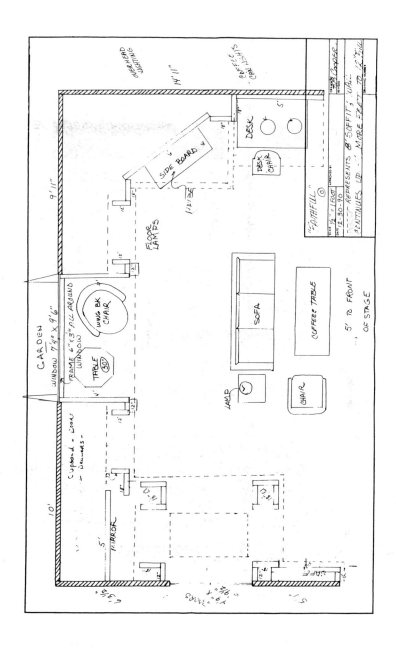

THE FILM SOCIETY
Jon Robin Baitz
(Little Theatre) Dramatic comedy
4m., 2f. Various ints. (may be unit set)

Imagine the best of Simon Gray crossed with the best of Athol Fugard. The New York critics lavished praise upon this wonderful play, calling Mr. Baitz a major new voice in our theatre. *The Film Society*, set in South Africa, is *not* about the effects of apartheid—at least, overtly. Blenheim is a provincial private school modeled on the second-rate British education machine. It is 1970, a time of complacency for everyone but Terry, a former teacher at Blenheim, who has lost his job because of his connections with Blacks (he invited a Black priest to speak at commencement). Terry tries to involve Jonathan, another teacher at the school and the central character in this play; but Jonathan cares only about his film society, which he wants to keep going at all costs—even if it means programming only safe, non-objectionable, films. When Jonathan's mother, a local rich lady, promises to donate a substantial amount of money to Blenheim if Jonathan is made Headmaster, he must finally choose which side he is on: Terry's or The Establishment's. "Using the school as a microcosm for South Africa, Baitz explores the psychological workings of repression in a society that has to kill its conscience in order to persist in a course of action it knows enough to abhor but cannot afford to relinquish."—New Yorker. "What distinguishes Mr. Baitz' writing, aside from its manifest literacy, is its ability to embrace the ambiguities of political and moral dilemmas that might easily be reduced to blacks and whites."—N.Y. Times. "A beautiful, accomplished play . . . things I thought I was a churl still to value or expect—things like character, plot and theatre dialogue—really do matter."—N.Y. Daily News. (#8123)

THE SUBSTANCE OF FIRE
Jon Robin Baitz
(Little Theatre.) Drama
3m., 2f. 2 Ints.

Isaac Geldhart, the scion of a family-owned publisher in New York which specializes in scholarly books, suddenly finds himself under siege. His firm is under imminent threat of a corporate takeover, engineered by his own son, Aaron, who watches the bottom line and sees the firm's profitability steadily declining. Aaron wants to publish a trashy novel which will certainly bring in the bucks; whereas Isaac wants to go on publishing worthy scholarly efforts such as his latest project, a multi-volume history of Nazi medical experiments during the Holocaust. Aaron has the bucks to effectively wrench control of the company from his father—or, rather, he has the yen (Japanese businessmen are backing him). What he needs are the votes of the other minority shareholders: his brother Martin and sister Sarah. Like Aaron, they have lived their lives under the thumb of Isaac's imperiousness; and, reluctantly, they agree to side with Aaron against the old man. In the second act, we are back in the library of Isaac's townhouse, a few years later. Isaac has been forcibly retired and has gotten so irascible and eccentric that he may possibly be *non compos mentis*. His children think so, which is why they have asked a psychiatric social worker from the court to interview Isaac to judge his competence. Isaac, who has survived the Holocaust and the death of his wife to build an important publishing company from scratch, must now face his greatest challenge—to persuade Marge Hackett that he is sane. "A deeply compassionate play."—N.Y. Times. "A remarkably intelligent drama. Baitz assimilates and refracts this intellectual history without stinting either on heart or his own original vision."—N.Y. Newsday. (#21379)

Other Publications for Your Interest

THE BALLAD OF SOAPY SMITH
(ADVANCED GROUPS—EPIC COMIC DRAMA)
By MICHAEL WELLER

24 men, 9 women (with doubling)—Various interiors and exteriors (may be unit set)

"Col." Jefferson Randolph Smith, known as "Soapy" to his friends and foes, is a celebrated, notorious con man whose reputation has, alas, not preceded him to the Alaska Gold Rush town of Skagway in 1897, when the play takes place. Soapy is a charming gentleman, and he starts up a protection racket which brings law and order to the town, giving it a church and an infirmary. Oddly enough Soapy, the criminal, becomes a force for moral good; until the town's hypocrisy and vicious self interest bring him down, a victim of the cardinal sin of believing in his own con. "Michael Weller deserves praise for a historical play with contemporary relevance, daring to accost a large canvas. The protagonist is a complex and absorbing creation. I left the theatre, for once, thinking rather than trying to forget."—N.Y. Mag. "A rousing epic"—AP. "A good time on a grand scale, with a mind and vision of rare intensity."—Gannett/Westchester Newsp.   (#3975)

HURLYBURLY
(ADVANCED GROUPS—DRAMA)
By DAVID RABE

4 men, 3 women—Interior

This rivetting new drama by the author of *The Basic Training of Pavlo Hummel, Sticks and Bones* and *Streamers* took New York by storm in a production directed by Mike Nichols and starring William Hurt, Sigourney Weaver, Judith Ivey, Christopher Walken, Harvey Keitel and Jerry Stiller. Quite a cast, and quite a play! The drama is the story of four men nosedeep in the decadent, perverted, cocaine-laden culture that is Hollywood; pursuing their sex-crazed, dope-ridden vision of the American Dream. "*Hurlyburly* offers some of Mr. Rabe's most inventive and disturbing writing. At his impressive best, Mr. Rabe makes grim, ribald and surprisingly compassionate comedy out of the lies and rationalizations that allow his alienated men to keep functioning (if not feeling) in the fogs of lotusland. They work in an industry so corrupt that its only honest executives are those who openly admit that they lie."—N.Y. Times. "Rabe has written a strange, bitterly funny, self-indulgent, important play."—N.Y. Post. "An important work, masterly accomplished."—Time. "A powerful permanent contribution to American drama . . . rivetting, disturbing, fearsomely funny . . . has a savage sincerity and a crackling theatrical vitality. This deeply felt play deserves as wide an audience as possible."—Newsweek.   (#10163)

Other Publications for Your Interest

LAKEBOAT
(ADVANCED GROUPS—COMEDY)